TEXAS TEST PREP

Student Quiz Book

STAAR Math

Grade 4

ISBN 978- 1463572853

CONTENTS

INTRODUCTION
For Parents, Teachers, and Tutors

STAAR Math Skills

Every grade 4 student in Texas is taught the same set of math skills. The set of skills that students are taught are described in the TEKS Student Expectations. These expectations list all the skills and knowledge that grade 4 students are expected to have. All grade 4 students are taught based on these skills, and then tested on these skills in the STAAR test.

Skill by Skill

In this book, each quiz tests one specific skill. There is one quiz for every skill that grade 4 students need to have. The TEKS Student Expectations are included at the back of the book, linking each quiz to the skill that it covers.

Preparing for the STAAR

This quiz book contains questions just like students will find on the STAAR math test. The questions have the same types, the same difficulty level, and test all the same skills. This quiz book is an effective way for students to prepare for taking the STAAR throughout the year. They will become familiar with answering STAAR questions, but can focus on understanding one skill at a time. This book can also be used to target gaps in knowledge and focus on improving a student's areas of weakness.

If the student can master the quizzes in this book, they will be prepared and ready to master the STAAR mathematics test.

Prepare Throughout the Year

The math skills in this book will all be learned by grade 4 students throughout the year. As students learn each skill, use the appropriate quiz for revision and to get the student used to answering STAAR questions on the skill. At the end of the year, take the mixed quizzes in this book as extra revision.

Score Tracker

As each quiz is scored, complete the Score Tracker in the back of the book. Total the scores once each section is complete to understand the student's strengths and weaknesses. Then target instruction and revision accordingly.

STAAR MATH

GRADE 4

QUIZ BOOK

Instructions

The quizzes contain multiple-choice questions. Read each question carefully. Then select the best answer. Fill in the circle for the correct answer.

You can use the mathematic chart on the next page to help you with some of the questions.

MATHEMATICS CHART

You may use this chart to help you answer questions in the test.

LENGTH

Metric
1 meter = 100 centimeters
1 centimeter = 10 millimeters

Customary
1 yard = 3 feet
1 foot = 12 inches

CAPACITY AND VOLUME

Metric
1 liter = 1000 milliliters

Customary
1 gallon = 4 quarts
1 gallon = 128 fluid ounces
1 quart = 2 pints
1 pint = 2 cups
1 cup = 8 fluid ounces

MASS AND WEIGHT

Metric
1 kilogram = 1000 grams
1 gram = 1000 milligrams

Customary
1 ton = 2000 pounds
1 pound = 16 ounces

TIME

Metric
1 year = 365 days
1 year = 12 months
1 year = 52 weeks

Customary
1 week = 7 days
1 day = 24 hours
1 hour = 60 minutes

QUIZ 1: Reading and Comparing Whole Numbers

1   There are 10,028 people in Errol's town. Which of these is another way to write 10,028?

    Ⓐ   1 + 2 + 8

    Ⓑ   100 + 2 + 8

    Ⓒ   10,000 + 20 + 8

    Ⓓ   10,000 + 2 + 8

2   Which of the following is another way to write the numeral 8,900,045?

    Ⓐ   Eight million, nine hundred thousand, forty-five

    Ⓑ   Eight hundred thousand, nine hundred and forty-five

    Ⓒ   Eight million, nine hundred and forty-five

    Ⓓ   Eight thousand, nine hundred, forty-five

3   Which digit is in the ten thousands place in the number 30,659,823?

    Ⓐ   3

    Ⓑ   5

    Ⓒ   9

    Ⓓ   2

QUIZ 1: Reading and Comparing Whole Numbers

4   Which number has a 7 in the millions place?

   Ⓐ   758,310,386

   Ⓑ   835,768,950

   Ⓒ   237,082,663

   Ⓓ   278,935,159

5   Which number is between 3,246 and 6,951?

   Ⓐ   5,673

   Ⓑ   9,368

   Ⓒ   2,784

   Ⓓ   3,190

6   The table shows the number of sales a store had on four days.

Monday	Tuesday	Wednesday	Thursday
4,087	4,155	4,001	3,995

Which list shows the days in order from least to greatest number of sales?

   Ⓐ   Thursday, Wednesday, Monday, Tuesday

   Ⓑ   Wednesday, Tuesday, Monday, Thursday

   Ⓒ   Wednesday, Monday, Tuesday, Thursday

   Ⓓ   Thursday, Monday, Tuesday, Wednesday

QUIZ 2: Reading and Comparing Decimals

1 Which decimal represents the shaded model below?

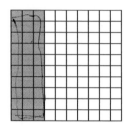

   Ⓐ   0.3

   Ⓑ   0.03

   Ⓒ   0.15

   Ⓓ   0.1

2 Which decimal represents the shaded model below?

   Ⓐ   1.8

   Ⓑ   0.08

   Ⓒ   8.0

   Ⓓ   0.8

3 Which shaded model represents 1.5?

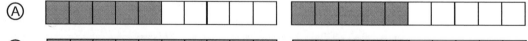

QUIZ 2: Reading and Comparing Decimals

4   Which decimal represents the shaded model below?

 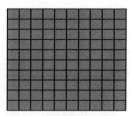 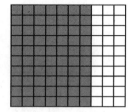

Write your answer on the line below.

_____

5   The two models below represent two decimals.

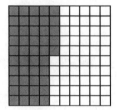 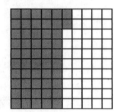

Which of the following compares the two decimals?

Ⓐ   0.45 > 0.52

Ⓑ   0.45 < 0.52

Ⓒ   4.5 > 5.2

Ⓓ   4.5 < 5.2

6   Which shaded model represents the smallest decimal?

Ⓐ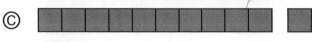

Ⓑ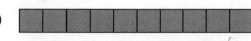

Ⓒ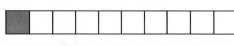

Ⓓ

QUIZ 3: Creating Equivalent Fractions

1 Which model is shaded to show a fraction equivalent to $\frac{6}{8}$?

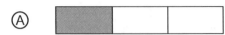

2 The shaded model below represents a fraction.

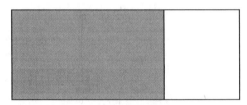

Which shaded model below represents an equivalent fraction?

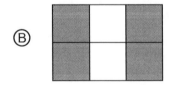

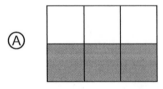

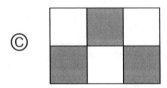

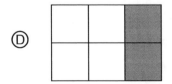

QUIZ 3: Creating Equivalent Fractions

3 Which fraction is **NOT** equivalent to the shaded area of the circle?

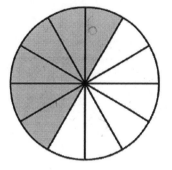

Ⓐ $\dfrac{6}{8}$

Ⓑ $\dfrac{1}{2}$

Ⓒ $\dfrac{6}{12}$

Ⓓ $\dfrac{2}{4}$

4 Which fraction is equivalent to the shaded area of the rectangle?

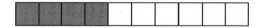

Ⓐ $\dfrac{4}{6}$

Ⓑ $\dfrac{2}{10}$

Ⓒ $\dfrac{2}{3}$

Ⓓ $\dfrac{2}{5}$

QUIZ 4: Modeling Fractions Greater than One

1   Which fraction does the shaded model represent?

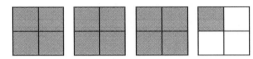

   Ⓐ $3\dfrac{3}{4}$

   Ⓑ $3\dfrac{1}{4}$

   Ⓒ $3\dfrac{1}{16}$

   Ⓓ $3\dfrac{1}{3}$

2   Which fraction does the model below represent?

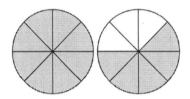

Write your answer on the line below.

_____

3   Which shaded model represents $3\dfrac{1}{2}$?

QUIZ 4: Modeling Fractions Greater than One

4 Which fraction does the shaded model below represent?

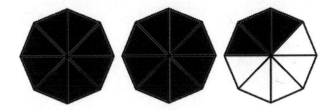

Ⓐ $2\dfrac{3}{5}$

Ⓑ $2\dfrac{1}{3}$

Ⓒ $2\dfrac{1}{2}$

Ⓓ $2\dfrac{3}{8}$

5 Which fraction does the shaded model below represent?

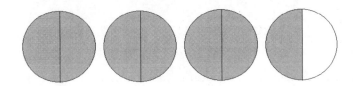

Ⓐ $\dfrac{7}{8}$

Ⓑ $\dfrac{7}{2}$

Ⓒ $\dfrac{3}{2}$

Ⓓ $\dfrac{8}{7}$

QUIZ 5: Comparing and Ordering Fractions

1   Which shaded model shows a fraction less than $\frac{2}{5}$?

2   The diagram below shows two sets of black and white stars.

Which of these compares the portion of black stars in each set?

Ⓐ $\frac{1}{3} > \frac{5}{9}$

Ⓑ $\frac{1}{3} < \frac{5}{9}$

Ⓒ $\frac{1}{3} < \frac{5}{3}$

Ⓓ $\frac{3}{6} > \frac{5}{4}$

3   Which set of squares has more than half of the squares shaded?

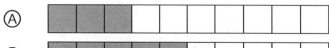

QUIZ 5: Comparing and Ordering Fractions

4   What do the shaded models below show?

 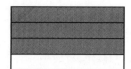

Ⓐ $\dfrac{4}{10} > \dfrac{1}{3}$

Ⓑ $\dfrac{5}{8} = \dfrac{3}{4}$

Ⓒ $\dfrac{10}{16} < \dfrac{3}{4}$

Ⓓ $\dfrac{3}{4} < \dfrac{1}{2}$

5   The shaded models below represent two fractions.

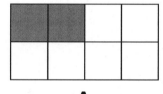

A   **B**

How much greater is fraction B than fraction A?

Ⓐ $\dfrac{5}{8}$

Ⓑ $\dfrac{3}{8}$

Ⓒ $\dfrac{1}{3}$

Ⓓ $\dfrac{2}{5}$

QUIZ 6: Relating Decimals to Fractions

1 The model below is shaded to show $1\frac{4}{10}$.

Write your answer on the line below.

_____

2 Which decimal does the shaded model below represent?

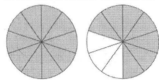

   Ⓐ   1.07

   Ⓑ   1.7

   Ⓒ   1.77

   Ⓓ   10.7

3 The model below is shaded to show $\frac{31}{100}$.

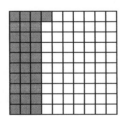

Which decimal does the model represent?

   Ⓐ   0.31

   Ⓑ   3.1

   Ⓒ   1.1

   Ⓓ   1.31

QUIZ 6: Relating Decimals to Fractions

4   Which model shows a fraction equivalent to 0.3?

Ⓐ

Ⓑ

Ⓒ

Ⓓ

5   The model below is shaded to show $2\frac{40}{100}$.

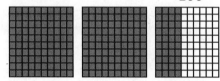

Which decimal does the model represent?

Ⓐ   0.24   Ⓒ   2.04

Ⓑ   2.4   Ⓓ   20.4

6   Which fraction does the shaded model below represent?

Ⓐ $2\frac{8}{100}$

Ⓑ $\frac{28}{100}$

Ⓒ $2\frac{8}{10}$

Ⓓ $2\frac{2}{10}$

QUIZ 7: Use Addition and Subtraction

1   Adam drove 295 miles on Saturday. Then he drove 243 miles on Sunday. How many miles did he drive in all? Write your answer on the line below.

_____

2   The table below shows the number of people who saw a play on Friday, Saturday, and Sunday night.

Night	Number of People
Friday	1,580
Saturday	1,898
Sunday	1,474

How many people in total went to see the play on the 3 nights?

Ⓐ   4,742

Ⓑ   4,752

Ⓒ   4,942

Ⓓ   4,952

3   The normal price of a car is $15,900. During a sale, the car is $1,499 less than the normal price. What is the sale price?

Ⓐ $14,401

Ⓑ $14,501

Ⓒ $14,509

Ⓓ $15,599

QUIZ 7: Use Addition and Subtraction

4 Emiko is starting a school where there are 247 students in grade 4. At her last school, there were 29 fewer students in grade 4. How many students were in grade 4 at Emiko's last school?

Ⓐ 218

Ⓑ 222

Ⓒ 266

Ⓓ 276

5 The table below shows the male and female population of Vale.

Gender	Population
Male	248,368
Female	267,182

What is the total population of Vale?

Ⓐ 405,540

Ⓑ 416,550

Ⓒ 505,440

Ⓓ 515,550

6 Simon has $896 in his savings account. He spent $179 on car repairs. How much money did Simon have left?

Ⓐ $717

Ⓑ $723

Ⓒ $985

Ⓓ $1,075

QUIZ 8: Add and Subtract Decimals

1 The decimal cards for 0.68 and 0.31 are shown below.

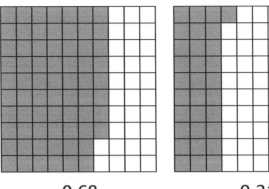

What is the sum of 0.68 and 0.31?

Ⓐ 0.91

Ⓑ 0.98

Ⓒ 0.99

Ⓓ 1.00

2 Sarah ran 1.8 miles on Monday and 2.6 miles on Tuesday. How many miles did Sarah run in all?

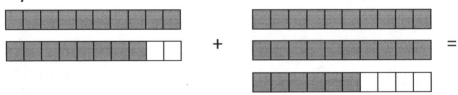

Ⓐ 3.4 miles

Ⓑ 4.0 miles

Ⓒ 4.4 miles

Ⓓ 4.6 miles

QUIZ 8: Add and Subtract Decimals

3   The decimal strips for 0.6 and 0.3 are shown below.

What is the difference of 0.6 and 0.3? Write your answer on the line below.

_____

4   Jacky had a piece of ribbon that was 2.4 meters long. She cut off a piece of ribbon that was 0.8 meters long. How much ribbon was left?

    Ⓐ   0.6 meters

    Ⓑ   1.6 meters

    Ⓒ   3.2 meters

    Ⓓ   4.2 meters

5   Chan had $2.90. He spent $1.98. How much did Chan have left?

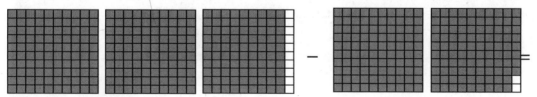

    Ⓐ $0.08

    Ⓑ $0.92

    Ⓒ $1.02

    Ⓓ $1.92

QUIZ 9: Model Factors and Products

1   Which number is represented by the grid below?

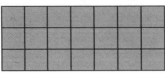

  Ⓐ   7

  Ⓑ   10

  Ⓒ   21

  Ⓓ   30

2   Which number sentence represents the array shown below?

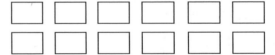

  Ⓐ $6 + 2 = 8$

  Ⓑ $6 \times 6 = 36$

  Ⓒ $6 \times 2 = 12$

  Ⓓ $20 - 8 = 12$

3   A 9 by 4 array is shown below.

What is the product of 9 and 4?

  Ⓐ   13

  Ⓑ   26

  Ⓒ   36

  Ⓓ   54

QUIZ 9: Model Factors and Products

4　Which diagram shows an array for the number 18?

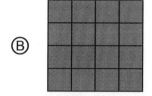

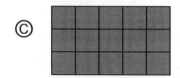

5　An array for the number 28 is shown below.

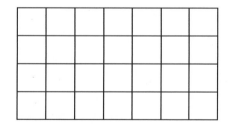

Which number is a factor of 28?

Ⓐ　3

Ⓑ　5

Ⓒ　7

Ⓓ　11

QUIZ 10: Represent Multiplication and Division

1 Jordana bought 4 packets of 20 cookies. Which number sentence can be used to find the total number of cookies?

 Ⓐ $20 + 4 =$ ☐

 Ⓑ $20 ÷ 5 =$ ☐

 Ⓒ $20 × 4 =$ ☐

 Ⓓ $20 - 4 =$ ☐

2 Lori is packing cans into boxes. She can fit 24 cans in each box. She has 360 cans to pack. Which number sentence can be used to find the total number of boxes she will need?

 Ⓐ $360 - 24 =$ ☐

 Ⓑ $360 + 24 =$ ☐

 Ⓒ $360 × 24 =$ ☐

 Ⓓ $360 ÷ 24 =$ ☐

3 Ronald has 12 dimes. He sorts them into 3 equal groups. How could you work out how many coins were in each group?

 Ⓐ Divide 12 by 3

 Ⓑ Multiply 3 by 12

 Ⓒ Add 12 and 3

 Ⓓ Subtract 3 from 12

QUIZ 10: Represent Multiplication and Division

4   Marita bought 8 bags of flour. There were 4 pounds of flour in each bag. Which number sentence can be used to find how many pounds of flour Marita bought?

Ⓐ $8 - 4 = \square$

Ⓑ $8 + 4 = \square$

Ⓒ $8 \times 4 = \square$

Ⓓ $8 \div 4 = \square$

5   Matt earns $8 per hour at his part-time job. He worked 24 hours in one week. How could you work out how much he earned?

Ⓐ   Divide 24 by 8

Ⓑ   Multiply 8 by 24

Ⓒ   Add 24 and 8

Ⓓ   Subtract 8 from 24

6   Jo has 18 star-shaped stickers. He places them in 3 even columns. Which of these shows how many stickers are in each row?

Ⓐ   ☆☆☆

Ⓑ   ☆☆☆☆☆☆☆☆

Ⓒ   ☆☆☆☆☆

Ⓓ   ☆☆☆☆☆

Quiz 11: Use Multiplication Facts

1   What is the product of 9 and 7?

Ⓐ   54

Ⓑ   56

Ⓒ   63

Ⓓ   72

2   What is the product of 6 and 12?

Ⓐ   60

Ⓑ   72

Ⓒ   78

Ⓓ   84

3   What is the product of 3 and 11?

Ⓐ   30

Ⓑ   31

Ⓒ   33

Ⓓ   36

4   What is the product of 8 and 8?

Ⓐ   36

Ⓑ   56

Ⓒ   64

Ⓓ   72

Quiz 11: Use Multiplication Facts

5   Max has 4 fish. He feeds each fish 5 food pellets per day. How many food pellets does he use each day?

 Ⓐ 16

 Ⓑ 20

 Ⓒ 25

 Ⓓ 40

6   Belle is putting baseball cards in an album. She can fit 12 baseball cards on each page. How many cards can she fit on 8 pages?

 Ⓐ 84

 Ⓑ 92

 Ⓒ 96

 Ⓓ 98

7   Kane is cutting oranges into wedges. He cuts each orange into 6 wedges. How many wedges will he have if he uses 7 oranges?

 Ⓐ 32

 Ⓑ 36

 Ⓒ 38

 Ⓓ 42

QUIZ 12: Solve Multiplication Problems

1   Louisa is making fruit punch. She pours 4 cartons of orange juice into the punch. Each carton contains 12 ounces of orange juice. How many ounces of orange juice were in the punch?

    Ⓐ   46

    Ⓑ   48

    Ⓒ   52

    Ⓓ   58

2   Alex saw the sign below at a fruit stand.

If Alex spent $3 on apples, how many apples would he get?

    Ⓐ   30

    Ⓑ   35

    Ⓒ   45

    Ⓓ   60

3   A music school divided its students into 5 classes. There were 19 students in each class. How many students were there in all?

    Ⓐ   38

    Ⓑ   55

    Ⓒ   90

    Ⓓ   95

QUIZ 12: Solve Multiplication Problems

4 An apple pie can be cut into 8 pieces. A restaurant makes 18 apple pies. How many pieces of apple pie can the restaurant sell?

Ⓐ 84

Ⓑ 116

Ⓒ 144

Ⓓ 160

5 Erin goes to a piano lesson each week. Each lesson goes for 90 minutes. How long does Erin spend at piano lessons in 4 weeks?

Ⓐ 270 minutes

Ⓑ 360 minutes

Ⓒ 2,700 minutes

Ⓓ 3,600 minutes

6 Kym is buying cotton to make curtains. The cotton costs $12 per yard. Kym buys 16 yards of cotton. How much would Kym pay for the cotton?

Ⓐ $82

Ⓑ $144

Ⓒ $168

Ⓓ $192

QUIZ 13: Solve Division Problems

1 Jodie needs to buy 42 cans of drink for a party. The cans of drink are sold in packs of 6. How many packs does Jodie need to buy?

   Ⓐ   5

   Ⓑ   6

   Ⓒ   7

   Ⓓ   8

2 Joseph earns $8 per hour. In one week, he earned $280. How many hours did Joseph work that week?

   Ⓐ   25 hours

   Ⓑ   30 hours

   Ⓒ   35 hours

   Ⓓ   40 hours

3 Samantha has a packet containing 80 candies. She wants to divide them evenly between 9 people. How many whole pieces of candy will each person receive?

   Ⓐ   8

   Ⓑ   9

   Ⓒ   10

   Ⓓ   12

QUIZ 13: Solve Division Problems

4   A factory has 42 workers. They want to divide the workers evenly into 3 different shifts. How many workers will be on each shift?

Ⓐ   12

Ⓑ   14

Ⓒ   16

Ⓓ   18

5   Mia is sorting her dimes into piles. She puts the dimes in piles of 5. She has a total of 85 dimes.

How many piles of dimes would Mia have?

Ⓐ   11

Ⓑ   13

Ⓒ   16

Ⓓ   17

6   A café has tables that each can seat 4 people. The café can seat a total of 112 people. How many tables does the café have?

Ⓐ   24

Ⓑ   26

Ⓒ   28

Ⓓ   29

QUIZ 14: Rounding and Estimating

1 May has 682 coins. Ali has 436 coins. Which number sentence shows the best way to estimate the total number of coins?

Ⓐ $600 + 400 = \square$

Ⓑ $600 + 500 = \square$

Ⓒ $700 + 400 = \square$

Ⓓ $700 + 500 = \square$

2 Which is the best estimate of how much greater the population of Milton is compared to Mayfair?

Town	Population
Mayfair	17,901
Milton	22,182
Lexington	27,855

Ⓐ 4,000

Ⓑ 5,000

Ⓒ 9,000

Ⓓ 10,000

3 The list shows how many cans each class collected.

Miss Adams   68
Mr. Walsh   52
Mrs. Naroda   37

Which is the best estimate of the number of cans collected in all?

Ⓐ 140   Ⓒ 160

Ⓑ 150   Ⓓ 170

QUIZ 14: Rounding and Estimating

4 Which 2 people have a combined age of about 40?

Name	Age
Rebecca	11
Anthony	16
Leah	22
Toby	27
Royston	7

Ⓐ Royston and Leah

Ⓑ Rebecca and Toby

Ⓒ Anthony and Royston

Ⓓ Toby and Leah

5 A theater has 497 seats. People are sitting in 352 of the seats. Which is the best estimate of the number of empty seats?

Ⓐ 50   Ⓒ 150

Ⓑ 100   Ⓓ 200

6 A mail carrier delivered 2,482 letters in the morning and 578 letters in the afternoon. Which is the best estimate of the number of letters delivered in all?

Ⓐ 2,500

Ⓑ 2,600

Ⓒ 2,900

Ⓓ 3,100

QUIZ 15: Estimating Division and Multiplication

1 A train travels 68 miles in 1 hour. If the train travels at the same speed, which is the best way to estimate how many miles the train travels in 4 hours?

Ⓐ $70 \times 4 = 280$

Ⓑ $65 \times 4 = 260$

Ⓒ $70 \times 5 = 350$

Ⓓ $60 \times 5 = 300$

2 Cans of chicken soup are sold in boxes of 24. A grocery store ordered 185 boxes of chicken soup. Which is the best estimate of the number of cans of chicken soup ordered?

Ⓐ   2,000

Ⓑ   3,000

Ⓒ   4,000

Ⓓ   6,000

3 An online bookstore sells 18 books every hour. At this rate, about how many books will the bookstore sell in 8 hours?

Ⓐ   30

Ⓑ   75

Ⓒ   100

Ⓓ   160

QUIZ 15: Estimating Division and Multiplication

4 Becky typed 1,294 words in 32 minutes. Which is the best way to estimate how many words Becky typed each minute?

Ⓐ 1200 ÷ 30 = 40

Ⓑ 1200 ÷ 40 = 30

Ⓒ 1000 ÷ 40 = 25

Ⓓ 1300 ÷ 50 = 26

5 A car traveled 189 miles in 3 hours. About how many miles did the car travel each hour?

Ⓐ 45 miles

Ⓑ 50 miles

Ⓒ 60 miles

Ⓓ 67 miles

6 Victor sent a total of 96 text messages in 1 month. Which is the best estimate of how many text messages he sent each day?

Ⓐ 3

Ⓑ 5

Ⓒ 25

Ⓓ 30

QUIZ 16: Multiplication and Division Facts

1 Which number sentence is in the same fact family as $11 \times 12 = 132$?

   Ⓐ $132 \div 4 = 33$

   Ⓑ $11 \times 11 = 121$

   Ⓒ $132 \div 12 = 11$

   Ⓓ $6 \times 22 = 132$

2 Which number sentence is **NOT** in the same fact family as $7 \times \square = 63$?

   Ⓐ $63 \div 7 = \square$

   Ⓑ $\square \times 7 = 63$

   Ⓒ $63 \div \square = 7$

   Ⓓ $7 \times 63 = \square$

3 There were 90 roses planted in a garden. There were 15 roses in each row. Which number sentence is in the same fact family as $90 \div 15 = \square$?

   Ⓐ $90 + 15 = \square$

   Ⓑ $\square \times 15 = 90$

   Ⓒ $90 - \square = 15$

   Ⓓ $15 \times 90 = \square$

QUIZ 16: Multiplication and Division Facts

4 In which number sentence does the number 4 make the equation true?

Ⓐ $24 \div \square = 6$

Ⓑ $\square \div 6 = 24$

Ⓒ $24 \times 6 = \square$

Ⓓ $\square \times 24 = 6$

5 Which number makes the number sentence below true?

$$\square \div 3 = 6$$

Ⓐ   9

Ⓑ   12

Ⓒ   18

Ⓓ   24

6 In which number sentence does the number 7 make the equation true?

Ⓐ $24 \div \square = 6$

Ⓑ $36 \div \square = 6$

Ⓒ $42 \div \square = 6$

Ⓓ $48 \div \square = 6$

QUIZ 17: Multiplying by 10 and 100

1 Which pair of numbers completes the equation below?

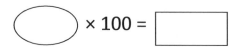

Ⓐ (91) and | 91,000 |

Ⓑ (91) and | 910 |

Ⓒ (910) and | 9,100 |

Ⓓ (910) and | 91,000 |

2 A box of nails contains 100 nails. Maxwell buys 12 boxes of nails. How many nails did Maxwell buy? Write your answer on the line below.

_____

3 There were 80 students in a fitness class. They were divided into groups of 10. Which number sentence is in the same fact family as $80 \div 10 = \square$?

Ⓐ $8 \times 80 = \square$

Ⓑ $\square \times 80 = 10$

Ⓒ $80 \times 10 = \square$

Ⓓ $\square \times 8 = 80$

QUIZ 17: Multiplying by 10 and 100

4 Which pair of numbers best completes this table?

Number	Number × 100
620	62,000
751	75,100
906	90,600

Ⓐ

250	2,500

Ⓑ

309	39,000

Ⓒ

541	54,100

Ⓓ

282	20,082

5 Joanna is making picture frames to sell at a market. She needs 10 feet of timber to make each frame. If she wants to make 18 timber frames, how many feet of timber will she need?

Ⓐ 28 feet

Ⓑ 108 feet

Ⓒ 180 feet

Ⓓ 1,800 feet

6 Craig is putting pennies into piles of 100. Craig makes 25 piles of 100 pennies. How many pennies does Craig have in all?

Ⓐ 125   Ⓒ 2,050

Ⓑ 250   Ⓓ 2,500

QUIZ 18: Describing Relationships

1   The table below shows the total number of beads Simone uses to make different numbers of bracelets.

Number of Bracelets	Number of Beads
3	60
4	80
5	100

Which of the following describes the relationship in the table?

Ⓐ   Number of bracelets × 20 = total number of beads

Ⓑ   Number of bracelets × 60 = total number of beads

Ⓒ   Number of bracelets × 100 = total number of beads

Ⓓ   Number of bracelets × 5 = total number of beads

2   The table below shows the total number of chairs that are needed to go with different numbers of tables.

Number of Tables	Number of Chairs
4	24
6	36
10	60

Which of the following describes the relationship in the table?

Ⓐ   Number of tables ÷ 6 = number of chairs

Ⓑ   Number of tables × 6 = number of chairs

Ⓒ   Number of tables ÷ 4 = number of chairs

Ⓓ   Number of tables × 4 = number of chairs

QUIZ 18: Describing Relationships

3 Each number that was put into the number machine below changed according to a rule.

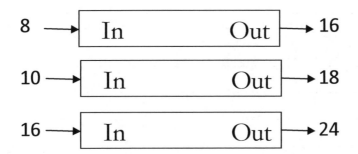

Which equation describes the rule for the number machine?

Ⓐ   Number in × 2 = number out

Ⓑ   Number in + 8 = number out

Ⓒ   Number in + 2 = number out

Ⓓ   Number in − 8 = number out

4 Each number in Set J is related in the same way to the number beside it in Set K.

Set J	Set K
2	6
5	15
7	21

When given a number in Set J, what is one way to find its related number in Set K?

Ⓐ   Multiply by 3   Ⓒ   Add 4

Ⓑ   Multiply by 5   Ⓓ   Add 10

QUIZ 19: Right, Acute, and Obtuse Angles

1 Look at the figure below.

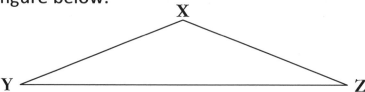

Which angles appear to be acute?

Ⓐ Angle X only

Ⓑ Angle Y only

Ⓒ Angle X and angle Z

Ⓓ Angle Y and angle Z

2 Which type of angle is shown below?

Write your answer on the line below.

_____

3 Which type of angle best describes angle S?

Ⓐ Acute

Ⓑ Obtuse

Ⓒ Straight

Ⓓ Right

QUIZ 19: Right, Acute, and Obtuse Angles

4   Which figure below appears to have at least one obtuse angle?

Ⓐ

Ⓑ

Ⓒ

Ⓓ

5   Which figure below has only right angles?

Ⓐ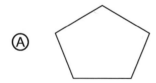

Ⓑ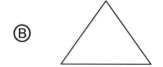

Ⓒ

Ⓓ

QUIZ 20: Parallel and Perpendicular Lines

1 Look at the line segments below.

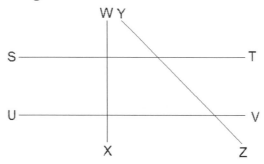

Which line segments appear to be parallel?

Ⓐ   WX and YZ

Ⓑ   ST and WX

Ⓒ   ST and UV

Ⓓ   UV and YZ

2 Look at the figure below.

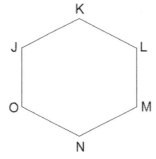

Which two sides of the figure appear to be parallel?

Ⓐ   KL and LM

Ⓑ   LM and ON

Ⓒ   OJ and JK

Ⓓ   KL and ON

QUIZ 20: Parallel and Perpendicular Lines

3   Which figure below has two sets of parallel sides?

Ⓐ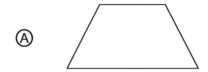

Ⓑ

Ⓒ

Ⓓ

4   Look at the line segments shown below.

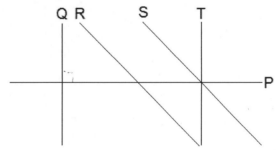

Which line segment is perpendicular to line Q?

Ⓐ   Line segment P

Ⓑ   Line segment R

Ⓒ   Line segment S

Ⓓ   Line segment T

QUIZ 21: Defining Geometric Figures

1 Which shape has more than 7 sides?

(A) Square

(B) Hexagon

(C) Octagon

(D) Pentagon

2 How many edges does the shape shown below have?

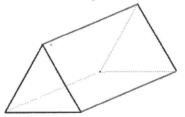

(A) 5

(B) 6

(C) 8

(D) 9

3 How many triangular faces does the square pyramid shown below have?

Write your answer on the line below.

_____

QUIZ 21: Defining Geometric Figures

4   Which shape has 6 square faces?

Ⓐ   Cube

Ⓑ   Rectangular prism

Ⓒ   Square pyramid

Ⓓ   Cylinder

5   Which of the following shapes is a trapezoid?

Ⓐ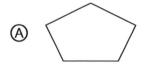

Ⓑ

Ⓒ

Ⓓ

6   How many vertices does the shape below have?

Ⓐ   1

Ⓑ   2

Ⓒ   4

Ⓓ   6

QUIZ 22: Translations, Reflections, and Rotations

1   Which single transformation could change Figure F to Figure G?

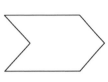 

            Figure F   Figure G

Ⓐ   Rotation

Ⓑ   Reflection

Ⓒ   Translation

Ⓓ   Not here

2   Which of the following diagrams shows a reflection?

Ⓐ

Ⓑ

Ⓒ

Ⓓ

QUIZ 22: Translations, Reflections, and Rotations

3 Which pair of figures shows a translation?

Ⓐ

Ⓑ

Ⓒ

Ⓓ

4 Which single transformation is shown below?

Ⓐ   Rotation

Ⓑ   Reflection

Ⓒ   Translation

Ⓓ   Not here

5 Which single transformation is shown below?

Ⓐ   Rotation

Ⓑ   Reflection

Ⓒ   Translation

Ⓓ   Not here

QUIZ 23: Identifying Symmetry

1 Which shape shown does **NOT** have a line of symmetry?

Ⓐ

Ⓑ

Ⓒ

Ⓓ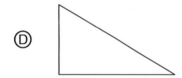

2 Which drawing shows a shape with a line of symmetry?

Ⓐ

Ⓑ

Ⓒ

Ⓓ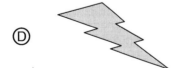

QUIZ 23: Identifying Symmetry

3   Which letter has 2 lines of symmetry?

    Ⓐ **H**

    Ⓑ **E**

    Ⓒ **L**

    Ⓓ **M**

4   How many lines of symmetry does the shape below have?

    Write your answer on the line below.

_____

5   Which diagram shows a line of symmetry?

    Ⓐ 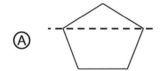

    Ⓑ 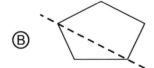

    Ⓒ 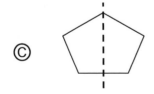

    Ⓓ 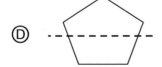

QUIZ 24: Locating Points on Number Lines

1   Which number does point *J* represent?

(A) $1\frac{1}{2}$

(B) $1\frac{1}{3}$

(C) $1\frac{1}{4}$

(D) $1\frac{1}{8}$

2   Which point on the number line represents 85?

(A)   Point *Q*

(B)   Point *R*

(C)   Point *S*

(D)   Point *T*

3   Which number does point *G* represent?

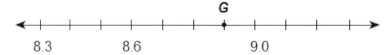

Write your answer on the line below.

_____

QUIZ 24: Locating Points on Number Lines

4 Which point on the number line represents 16.2?

Ⓐ Point *W*

Ⓑ Point *X*

Ⓒ Point *Y*

Ⓓ Point *Z*

5 Which number does point *S* represent?

Write your answer on the line below.

_____

6 Which point on the number line represents $2\frac{1}{2}$?

Ⓐ Point *K*

Ⓑ Point *L*

Ⓒ Point *M*

Ⓓ Point *N*

QUIZ 25: Estimating and Measuring

1 Which is the best estimate of the length of a shoe?

    Ⓐ   20 millimeters

    Ⓑ   20 meters

    Ⓒ   20 centimeters

    Ⓓ   20 kilometers

2 What is the perimeter of the square shown below?

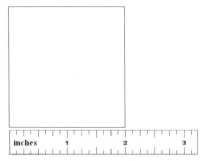

    Ⓐ   2 inches

    Ⓑ   4 inches

    Ⓒ   8 inches

    Ⓓ   12 inches

3 Which is the best estimate of the weight of a truck?

    Ⓐ   5 tons

    Ⓑ   500 pounds

    Ⓒ   5,000 grams

    Ⓓ   50 kilograms

QUIZ 25: Estimating and Measuring

4 Justin makes a cup of herb tea by adding hot water to a tea cup.

About how much water could Justin have added to the tea cup?

Ⓐ   200 milliliters

Ⓑ   200 pints

Ⓒ   200 liters

Ⓓ   200 quarts

5 Which unit would be best for finding the mass of a paperclip?

Ⓐ   Centimeters

Ⓑ   Milligrams

Ⓒ   Kilograms

Ⓓ   Meters

6 What is the area of the door mat shown below?

20 inches

30 inches

Ⓐ   50 square inches

Ⓑ   100 square inches

Ⓒ   400 square inches

Ⓓ   600 square inches

QUIZ 26: Converting Units

1 Alison bought a half gallon carton of milk. How many quarts of milk did the milk carton contain?

    Ⓐ   1 quart

    Ⓑ   2 quarts

    Ⓒ   4 quarts

    Ⓓ   8 quarts

2 Mrs. Masters added 2 liters of oil to her car. How many milliliters of oil did Mrs. Masters use?

    Ⓐ   20 milliliters

    Ⓑ   200 milliliters

    Ⓒ   2,000 milliliters

    Ⓓ   20,000 milliliters

3 Which measurement is the same as 4 yards?

    Ⓐ   12 feet

    Ⓑ   48 feet

    Ⓒ   12 inches

    Ⓓ   48 inches

QUIZ 26: Converting Units

4 Marcus competed in a marathon. He ran 42 kilometers. How many meters did Marcus run?

   Ⓐ   420 meters

   Ⓑ   4,200 meters

   Ⓒ   42,000 meters

   Ⓓ   420,000 meters

5 A pumpkin weighs 4 pounds. How many ounces does the pumpkin weigh?

   Ⓐ   32 ounces

   Ⓑ   40 ounces

   Ⓒ   48 ounces

   Ⓓ   64 ounces

6 A puppy weighed 6,000 grams. How many kilograms did the puppy weigh?

   Ⓐ   6 kilograms

   Ⓑ   60 kilograms

   Ⓒ   60,000 kilograms

   Ⓓ   6,000,000 kilograms

QUIZ 27: Measuring Volume

1 The model below was made with 1-inch cubes.

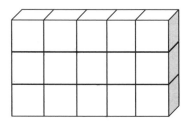

What is the volume of the model?

Ⓐ   15 cubic inches

Ⓑ   16 cubic inches

Ⓒ   20 cubic inches

Ⓓ   23 cubic inches

2 The model below was made with 1-unit cubes.

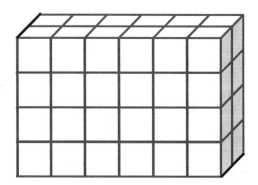

What is the volume of the model?

Ⓐ   24 cubic units

Ⓑ   36 cubic units

Ⓒ   44 cubic units

Ⓓ   48 cubic units

QUIZ 27: Measuring Volume

3   The model below was made with 1-cm cubes.

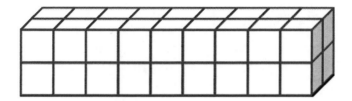

What is the volume of the model?

Ⓐ   18 cubic centimeters

Ⓑ   36 cubic centimeters

Ⓒ   72 cubic centimeters

Ⓓ   81 cubic centimeters

4   The cube shown below is 5 cubes wide, 5 cubes long, and 5 cubes deep.

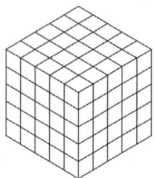

What is the volume of the cube?

Ⓐ   15 cubic units

Ⓑ   25 cubic units

Ⓒ   50 cubic units

Ⓓ   125 cubic units

QUIZ 28: Measuring Temperature

1   What temperature is shown on the thermometer below?

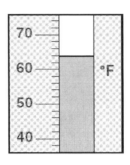

Ⓐ   62°F

Ⓑ   63°F

Ⓒ   64°F

Ⓓ   65°F

2   The thermometer below shows the temperature at noon.

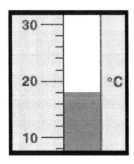

By 2 p.m., the temperature had risen by 8°C. What was the temperature at 2 p.m.?

Ⓐ   10°C

Ⓑ   11°C

Ⓒ   26°C

Ⓓ   27°C

QUIZ 28: Measuring Temperature

3   The thermometer below shows the air temperature in a refrigerator.

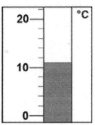

What temperature is shown?

Ⓐ   10°C

Ⓑ   11°C

Ⓒ   12°C

Ⓓ   15°C

4   The thermometers below show the low temperature for a day and the high temperature for a day.

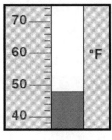   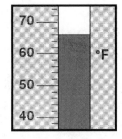

Low temperature   High temperature

How much greater was the high temperature than the low temperature?

Ⓐ   18°F

Ⓑ   20°F

Ⓒ   22°F

Ⓓ   66°F

QUIZ 29: Finding the Number of Combinations

1   The picture shows the types of shoes and socks that Jay has.

How many combinations of 1 pair of shoes and 1 pair of socks are possible?

Ⓐ   4

Ⓑ   6

Ⓒ   8

Ⓓ   16

2   Mick is ordering a baseball cap. The diagram below shows the sizes and colors available.

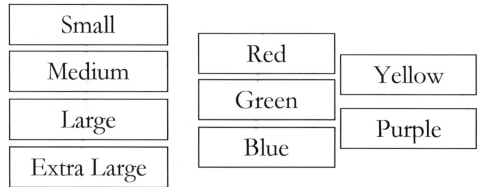

How many combinations of 1 size and 1 color are possible?

Ⓐ   9   Ⓒ   20

Ⓑ   16   Ⓓ   25

QUIZ 29: Finding the Number of Combinations

3 Rebecca is choosing writing paper. The picture below shows the patterns and the colors available.

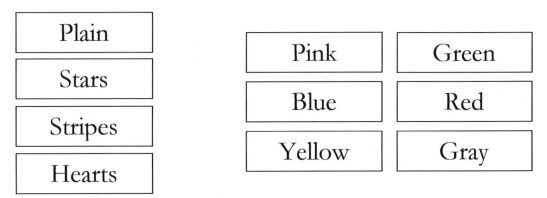

How many combinations of 1 pattern and 1 color are possible? Write your answer on the line below.

_____

4 Mrs. Porter is choosing dancing partners. The diagram below shows the boys and girls available.

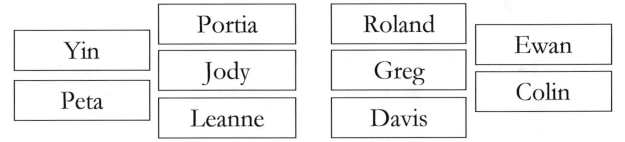

How many combinations of 1 boy and 1 girl are possible?

Ⓐ 5

Ⓑ 10

Ⓒ 20

Ⓓ 25

QUIZ 30: Interpreting Bar Graphs

The graph below shows how long Jason studied each week day. Use the graph to answer questions 1, 2, and 3.

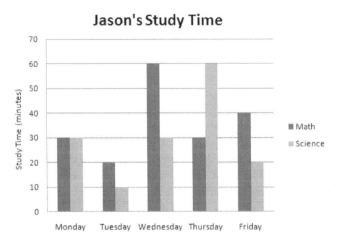

1   How long did Jason study science for on Wednesday? Write your answer on the line below.

_____

2   How long did Jason study for on Friday in all?

Ⓐ   20 minutes

Ⓑ   40 minutes

Ⓒ   60 minutes

Ⓓ   80 minutes

3   On which day did Jason study math for 20 minutes longer than science? Write your answer on the line below.

_____

QUIZ 30: Interpreting Bar Graphs

The graph below shows the number of points 6 players scored in a basketball game. Use the graph to answer questions 4, 5, and 6.

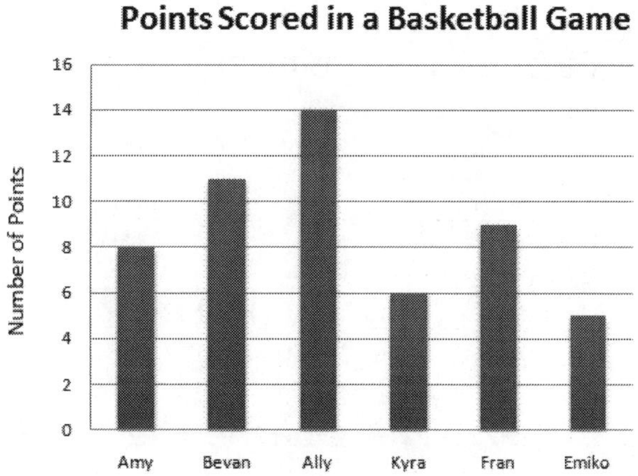

Points Scored in a Basketball Game

4   How many points did Fran score?

Ⓐ   6   Ⓒ   9

Ⓑ   8   Ⓓ   10

5   How many more points did Ally score than Emiko?

Ⓐ   9   Ⓒ   14

Ⓑ   10   Ⓓ   19

6   Which two players scored 20 points in total?

Ⓐ   Amy and Ally

Ⓑ   Bevan and Fran

Ⓒ   Kyra and Amy

Ⓓ   Ally and Emiko

QUIZ 31: Mathematics in Everyday Situations

1   Ryan bought a packet of nails for $3, a hammer for $8, and 6 large hooks. What information is needed to find the total amount Ryan spent?

Ⓐ   The price of each large hook

Ⓑ   The cost of the nails and the hammer together

Ⓒ   The amount of change he received

Ⓓ   The number of nails in a packet

2   Jolie is ordering pizzas for a party. The pizzas are $6 each. Jolie wants to order 8 pizzas. What other information is needed to find if Jolie has enough money to order 8 pizzas?

Ⓐ   How many slices each pizza has

Ⓑ   How much money Jolie has to spend

Ⓒ   How many guests the party has

Ⓓ   How much the 8 pizzas will cost

3   Sandra is buying yogurt at a store. Sandra saw this sign for a special deal on yogurt.

Yogurt
2 Tubs for $3

How many tubs of yogurt can Sandra buy for $9?

Ⓐ   3   Ⓒ   9

Ⓑ   6   Ⓓ   12

QUIZ 31: Mathematics in Everyday Situations

4   Mia is buying Christmas cards. She wants to send 38 Christmas cards. The cards come in packets of 5. How many packets would Mia need to buy to send 38 Christmas cards?

Ⓐ   6

Ⓑ   7

Ⓒ   8

Ⓓ   190

5   Mickey is buying school books. The total cost of the books is $42. The cashier tells Mickey he can have $10 off because he is a student. How can Mickey find out how much the books will cost after the discount?

Ⓐ   Subtract $10 from $42

Ⓑ   Add $10 to $42

Ⓒ   Divide $42 by $10

Ⓓ   Multiply $42 by $10

6   Jackson bought 6 lollipops for 15 cents each. How much change would Jackson receive from $1?

Write your answer on the line below.

_____

QUIZ 32: Solving Problems

1 Darren is 48 inches tall. Michael is 12 inches taller than Darren. How tall is Michael in feet?

Ⓐ   3 ft

Ⓑ   4 ft

Ⓒ   5 ft

Ⓓ   6 ft

2 The table below shows the entry cost for a zoo.

Adult	$12 per person
Child	$8 per person
Family (2 adults and 2 children)	$35 per family

How much would it cost for 2 adults and 1 child to go to the zoo?

Ⓐ $28

Ⓑ $32

Ⓒ $35

Ⓓ $40

3 It takes Liam from 4 to 6 weeks to read a novel. At this rate, about how long will it take Liam to read 5 novels?

Ⓐ   1 week

Ⓑ   15 weeks

Ⓒ   25 weeks

Ⓓ   50 weeks

QUIZ 32: Solving Problems

4   Bananas weigh between 3 and 5 ounces each. Donna bought 1 pound of bananas. About how many bananas did Donna buy?

Ⓐ   2 bananas

Ⓑ   4 bananas

Ⓒ   48 bananas

Ⓓ   64 bananas

5   Jane is making punch. She wants to make enough punch for each person to have 2 glasses. What other question needs to be answered to work out how much punch Jane should make?

Ⓐ   What sort of punch is Jane making?

Ⓑ   How many people are coming to the party?

Ⓒ   What is the party for?

Ⓓ   How much punch will Jane drink?

6   Bagels are sold in packets of 4 or packets of 6. Dom needs to buy exactly 20 bagels. Which set of packets could Dom buy?

Ⓐ   1 packet of 4 bagels and 3 packets of 6 bagels

Ⓑ   2 packets of 4 bagels and 2 packets of 6 bagels

Ⓒ   3 packets of 4 bagels and 2 packets of 6 bagels

Ⓓ   4 packets of 4 bagels and 1 packet of 6 bagels

QUIZ 33: Using Strategies to Solve Problems

1 Zoran is making muffins for a bake sale. Each muffin tray makes 12 muffins. Zoran wants to bake at least 80 muffins. How many trays of muffins will Zoran need to bake? Write your answer on the line below.

_____

2 Ellen selected a number. She followed the set of rules below.
  Divide the number by 2.
  Add 6 to the number.
  Multiply the number by 4.
The result was 40. What number did Ellen start with?

Ⓐ 2

Ⓑ 8

Ⓒ 104

Ⓓ 40

3 Reggie is recording the length of the major rivers in North America. Reggie wants to compare the lengths of the rivers. What would be the best way for Reggie to organize the information?

Ⓐ Make a table of the rivers and their lengths

Ⓑ Create a graph showing the longest and the shortest river

Ⓒ Add up the lengths of all the rivers

Ⓓ Highlight all the rivers on a map of the United States

QUIZ 33: Using Strategies to Solve Problems

4 The table below shows the cost of food at a diner.

Drinks		Meals	
Small milkshake	$1.80	Plain hamburger	$3.50
Large milkshake	$2.00	Chicken burger	$4.20
Small soda	$1.10	Hotdog	$2.50
Large soda	$1.50	Meatball sub	$3.10
Fruit juice	$1.90	Quiche	$2.10

Max has $5.00 to spend on lunch. Which two items could Max **NOT** buy?

Ⓐ Meatball sub and a fruit juice

Ⓑ Plain hamburger and a large soda

Ⓒ Large milkshake and a hotdog

Ⓓ Chicken burger and a small soda

5 What is the largest even number that can be made using the digits 3, 8, and 7? Each digit must be used only once in each number.

Ⓐ 873

Ⓑ 837

Ⓒ 378

Ⓓ 738

Quiz 34: Using Mathematical Language

1   Maria bought 10 new softball uniforms from a sports store. How can she find out the price of 1 softball uniform?

   Ⓐ   Divide the total cost by 10

   Ⓑ   Multiply the total cost by 10

   Ⓒ   Subtract 10 from the total cost

   Ⓓ   Add 10 to the total cost

2   There are 6 reams of paper in a box. Allison wants to order 30 reams of paper. Which of the following shows how to find the number of boxes of paper Allison should order?

   Ⓐ   Find the quotient of 30 and 6

   Ⓑ   Find the product of 30 and 6

   Ⓒ   Find the sum of 30 and 6

   Ⓓ   Find the difference between 30 and 6

3   Ty bought 3 shirts. He gave the cashier $30 and received $9 change. What is one way to find how much Ty paid for each shirt?

   Ⓐ   Add 30 to 9 and divide the result by 3

   Ⓑ   Subtract 9 from 30 and divide the result by 3

   Ⓒ   Add 30 to 9 and multiply the result by 3

   Ⓓ   Subtract 9 from 30 and multiply the result by 3

Quiz 34: Using Mathematical Language

4 Jessie saves $5 each week. Which number sentence can be used to find how many weeks it will take Jessie to save $40?

Ⓐ $40 - 5 = $ ☐

Ⓑ $40 + 5 = $ ☐

Ⓒ $40 \div 5 = $ ☐

Ⓓ $40 \times 5 = $ ☐

5 Sushi sells for $2 for each small roll and $4 for each large roll. Nora bought 1 small roll and 3 large rolls of sushi.

Which of these can be used to find the total cost of the sushi?

Ⓐ $2 + 12 = $ ☐

Ⓑ $2 \times 4 = $ ☐

Ⓒ $6 + 12 = $ ☐

Ⓓ $1 \times 8 = $ ☐

6 The high temperature on Sunday was 29°C. The high temperature on Monday was 33°C. The high temperature on Tuesday was 26°C. Which of these compares the high temperatures correctly?

Ⓐ $26 < 29 < 33$

Ⓑ $26 > 33 < 29$

Ⓒ $33 < 29 < 26$

Ⓓ $33 < 26 > 29$

QUIZ 35: Making Generalizations

1   Look at the group of numbers below.

925	851	792
543	699	776

What do these numbers have in common?

Ⓐ   They are all even numbers.

Ⓑ   They are all odd numbers.

Ⓒ   They are all greater than 500.

Ⓓ   They are all less than 900.

2   David drew these shapes.

Stella drew these shapes.

Which shape could be added to David's shapes?

Ⓐ

Ⓑ

Ⓒ

Ⓓ

QUIZ 35: Making Generalizations

3 Derryn grouped a set of numbers into the groups shown below.

Group 1	Group 2
105	421
855	869
325	326
790	784

Which number belongs in Group 1?

Ⓐ   246   Ⓒ   108

Ⓑ   630   Ⓓ   963

4 Which of the following describes the rule for this pattern?

2, 6, 3, 7, 4, 8, 5, 9, 6

Ⓐ   Add 4, divide by 2

Ⓑ   Add 4, subtract 3

Ⓒ   Multiply by 3, subtract 3

Ⓓ   Subtract 1, add 7

5 Beth wrote the set of expressions below.

$3 + 5$ 8×1 $4 + 4$ $10 - 2$

Which expression could be added to the set?

Ⓐ $6 - 4$

Ⓑ $1 + 8$

Ⓒ 10×2

Ⓓ $24 \div 3$

Quiz 36: Mixed Quiz A

1 Frankie is ordering a milkshake. The picture below shows the sizes and flavors available.

Small
Medium
Large

Chocolate	Caramel
Strawberry	Banana
Vanilla	Mango

How many combinations of 1 size and 1 flavor are possible?

Ⓐ 9

Ⓑ 12

Ⓒ 18

Ⓓ 36

2 Which digit is in the thousands place in the number 5,189,672?

Ⓐ 5

Ⓑ 1

Ⓒ 9

Ⓓ 6

3 What is the product of 6 and 8? Write your answer on the line below.

_____

Quiz 36: Mixed Quiz A

4 Ryan bought 8 fish. He paid $3 for each fish. How much did the 8 fish cost?

    Ⓐ $11

    Ⓑ $16

    Ⓒ $24

    Ⓓ $32

5 Travis collects coins. Travis had 459 coins in his collection. He gave 87 coins to his sister. Which number sentence shows the best way to estimate the number of coins Travis had left?

    Ⓐ $450 - 80 = \square$

    Ⓑ $450 - 90 = \square$

    Ⓒ $460 - 80 = \square$

    Ⓓ $460 - 90 = \square$

6 Which measurement is the same as 20 kilometers?

    Ⓐ   2,000 meters

    Ⓑ   20,000 meters

    Ⓒ   20,000 millimeters

    Ⓓ   200,000 millimeters

Quiz 37: Mixed Quiz B

1   Which is the best estimate of the length of a carrot?

   Ⓐ   20 millimeters

   Ⓑ   20 centimeters

   Ⓒ   20 meters

   Ⓓ   20 kilometers

2   There are 3 notepads in a packet. Allison wants to buy 12 notepads. Which of the following shows how to find the number of packets of notepads Allison should buy?

   Ⓐ   Find the quotient of 12 and 3

   Ⓑ   Find the product of 12 and 3

   Ⓒ   Find the sum of 12 and 3

   Ⓓ   Find the difference between 12 and 3

3   Becky is planning the seating for a wedding. There are a total of 92 wedding guests. Each table can seat 8 guests. How many tables will Becky need to seat all the guests?

   Ⓐ   8

   Ⓑ   9

   Ⓒ   11

   Ⓓ   12

Quiz 37: Mixed Quiz B

4 Maria earns $7 per hour at her part-time job. She worked 21 hours in one week. How could you work out how much she earned that week?

ⓐ   Divide 21 by 7

ⓑ   Multiply 7 by 21

ⓒ   Add 21 and 7

ⓓ   Subtract 7 from 21

5 Westmead School has 175 students in grade 4. The students are divided into classes of about 30 students each. What is the best estimate of the number of grade 4 classes?

ⓐ   5   ⓒ   7

ⓑ   6   ⓓ   8

6 The table below shows the number of people who saw a play on Friday, Saturday, and Sunday.

Day	Number of People
Friday	1,580
Saturday	1,898
Sunday	1,474

How many more people saw the play on Saturday than on Sunday?

ⓐ   424

ⓑ   318

ⓒ   1,424

ⓓ   434

Quiz 38: Mixed Quiz C

1   Each number that was put into the number machine below changed according to a rule.

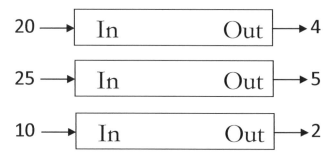

Which equation describes the rule for the number machine?

Ⓐ   Number in ÷ 5 = number out

Ⓑ   Number in + 16 = number out

Ⓒ   Number in × 5 = number out

Ⓓ   Number in − 8 = number out

2   Which model shows a fraction equivalent to 0.7?

3   Which letter has a line of symmetry?

Ⓐ   P   Ⓒ   S

Ⓑ   R   Ⓓ   T

Quiz 38: Mixed Quiz C

4   Look at the line segments below.

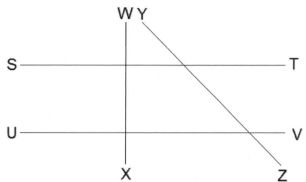

Which line segments appear to be perpendicular?

Ⓐ   WX and YZ

Ⓑ   ST and WX

Ⓒ   ST and UV

Ⓓ   UV and YZ

5   Which point on the number line represents 80?

Ⓐ   Point *Q*

Ⓑ   Point *R*

Ⓒ   Point *S*

Ⓓ   Point *T*

Quiz 39: Mixed Quiz D

1 How many pairs of parallel sides does the figure below have?

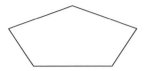

   Ⓐ   0

   Ⓑ   1

   Ⓒ   2

   Ⓓ   3

2 Which decimal represents the shaded model below?

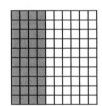

   Ⓐ   0.4

   Ⓑ   0.04

   Ⓒ   0.2

   Ⓓ   0.44

3 Which number makes the number sentence below true?

$$36 \div \square = 9$$

Write your answer on the line below.

_____

Quiz 39: Mixed Quiz D

4 Which pair of numbers completes the equation below?

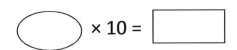 × 10 =

Ⓐ 63 and 6,300

Ⓑ 63 and 603

Ⓒ 630 and 6,300

Ⓓ 630 and 6,030

5 Which type of angle is shown below?

Ⓐ Acute

Ⓑ Obtuse

Ⓒ Straight

Ⓓ Right

6 How many faces does the rectangular prism shown below have?

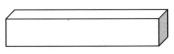

Ⓐ 3   Ⓒ 6

Ⓑ 4   Ⓓ 8

Quiz 40: Mixed Quiz E

1 What do the numbers below have in common?

266	98	166	20	522

Ⓐ   They are all even numbers.

Ⓑ   They are all odd numbers.

Ⓒ   They are all greater than 100.

Ⓓ   They are all less than 500.

2 What is the volume of the model shown below?

Ⓐ   8 cubic units

Ⓑ   12 cubic units

Ⓒ   18 cubic units

Ⓓ   24 cubic units

3 Which fraction is equivalent to the shaded area of the rectangle?

Ⓐ $\dfrac{4}{6}$

Ⓑ $\dfrac{2}{10}$

Ⓒ $\dfrac{2}{5}$

Ⓓ $\dfrac{1}{3}$

Quiz 40: Mixed Quiz E

4   Alvin selected a number. He followed the set of rules below.

Multiply the number by 4.
Add 2 to the number.
Divide the number by 2.

The result was 9. What number did Alvin start with?

Ⓐ   2

Ⓑ   4

Ⓒ   8

Ⓓ   10

5   Which model shows a fraction equivalent to 0.6?

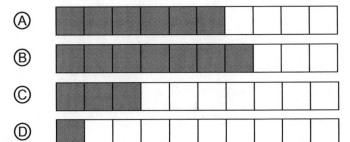

6   An array for the number 27 is shown below.

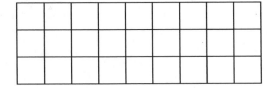

Which number is a factor of 27?

Ⓐ   2   Ⓒ   3

Ⓑ   6   Ⓓ   12

ANSWER KEY

QUIZ 1: Reading and Comparing Whole Numbers

1. C
2. A
3. B
4. C
5. A
6. A

QUIZ 2: Reading and Comparing Decimals

1. A
2. D
3. B
4. 2.7
5. B
6. D

QUIZ 3: Creating Equivalent Fractions

1. C
2. B
3. A
4. D

QUIZ 4: Modeling Fractions Greater than One

1. B
2. 1⅝
3. A
4. D
5. B

QUIZ 5: Comparing and Ordering Fractions

1. A
2. B
3. C
4. C
5. B

QUIZ 6: Relating Decimals to Fractions

1. 1.4
2. B
3. A
4. C
5. B
6. C

QUIZ 7: Use Addition and Subtraction

1. 538
2. D
3. A
4. A
5. D
6. A

QUIZ 8: Add and Subtract Decimals

1. C
2. C
3. 0.3
4. B
5. B

QUIZ 9: Model Factors and Products

1. C
2. C
3. C
4. A
5. C

QUIZ 10: Represent Multiplication and Division

1. C
2. D
3. A
4. C
5. B
6. C

QUIZ 11: Use Multiplication Facts

1. C
2. B
3. C
4. C
5. B
6. C
7. D

QUIZ 12: Solve Multiplication Problems

1. B
2. C
3. D
4. C
5. B
6. D

QUIZ 13: Solve Division Problems

1. C
2. C
3. A
4. B
5. D
6. C

QUIZ 14: Rounding and Estimating

1. C
2. A
3. C
4. B
5. C
6. D

QUIZ 15: Estimating Division and Multiplication

1. A
2. C
3. D
4. A
5. C
6. A

QUIZ 16: Multiplication and Division Facts

1. C
2. D
3. B
4. A
5. C
6. C

QUIZ 17: Multiplying by 10 and 100

1. D
2. 1,200
3. D
4. C
5. C
6. D

QUIZ 18: Describing Relationships

1. A
2. B
3. B
4. A

QUIZ 19: Right, Acute, and Obtuse Angles

1. D
2. Obtuse
3. A
4. A
5. C

QUIZ 20: Parallel and Perpendicular Lines

1. C
2. D
3. C
4. A

QUIZ 21: Defining Geometric Figures

1. C
2. D
3. 4
4. A
5. B
6. C

QUIZ 22: Translations, Reflections, and Rotations

1. A
2. C
3. A
4. B
5. C

QUIZ 23: Identifying Symmetry

1. D
2. B
3. A
4. 2
5. C

QUIZ 24: Locating Points on Number Lines

1. C
2. C
3. 8.9
4. A
5. 42
6. C

QUIZ 25: Estimating and Measuring

1. C
2. C
3. A
4. A
5. B
6. D

QUIZ 26: Converting Units

1. B
2. C
3. A
4. C
5. D
6. A

QUIZ 27: Measuring Volume

1. A
2. D
3. B
4. D

QUIZ 28: Measuring Temperature

1. C
2. C
3. B
4. A

QUIZ 29: Finding the Number of Combinations

1. C
2. C
3. 24
4. D

QUIZ 30: Interpreting Bar Graphs

1. 30 minutes
2. C
3. Friday
4. C
5. A
6. B

QUIZ 31: Mathematics in Everyday Situations

1. A
2. B
3. B
4. C
5. A
6. 10 cents

QUIZ 32: Solving Problems

1. C
2. B
3. C
4. B
5. B
6. B

QUIZ 33: Using Strategies to Solve Problems

1. 7
2. B
3. A
4. D
5. D

Quiz 34: Using Mathematical Language

1. A
2. A
3. B
4. C
5. A
6. A

Quiz 35: Making Generalizations

1. C
2. B
3. B
4. B
5. D

Quiz 36: Mixed Quiz A

1. C
2. C
3. 48
4. C
5. D
6. B

Quiz 37: Mixed Quiz B

1. B
2. A
3. D
4. B
5. B
6. A

Quiz 38: Mixed Quiz C

1. A
2. B
3. D
4. B
5. B

Quiz 39: Mixed Quiz D

1. A
2. A
3. 4
4. C
5. A
6. C

Quiz 40: Mixed Quiz E

1. A
2. D
3. A
4. B
5. A
6. C

TEKS STUDENT EXPECTATIONS

The STAAR test given by the state of Texas tests a specific set of skills and knowledge. The skills and knowledge tested are described in the TEKS Student Expectations, and are divided into 6 broad objectives. These expectations list all the skills and knowledge that grade 4 students are expected to have.

Quizzes 1 through 35 in this book each test one specific TEKS expectation. The table below lists the TEKS expectation covered by each quiz.

Objective 1: Numbers, Operations, and Quantitative Reasoning.		
Quiz 1	4.1 A	The student is expected to use place value to read, write, compare, and order whole numbers through 999,999,999.
Quiz 2	4.1 B	The student is expected to use place value to read, write, compare, and order decimals involving tenths and hundredths, including money, using pictorial models.
Quiz 3	4.2 A	The student is expected to use pictorial models to generate equivalent fractions.
Quiz 4	4.2 B	The student is expected to model fraction quantities greater than one using pictorial models.
Quiz 5	4.2 C	The student is expected to compare and order fractions using pictorial models.
Quiz 6	4.2 D	The student is expected to relate decimals to fractions that name tenths and hundredths using pictorial models.
Quiz 7	4.3 A	The student is expected to use addition and subtraction to solve problems involving whole numbers.
Quiz 8	4.3 B	The student is expected to add and subtract decimals to the hundredths place using pictorial models.
Quiz 9	4.4 A	The student is expected to model factors and products using arrays and area models.
Quiz 10	4.4 B	The student is expected to represent multiplication and division situations in picture, word, and number form.
Quiz 11	4.4 C	The student is expected to recall and apply multiplication facts through 12×12.

Quiz 12	4.4 D	The student is expected to use multiplication to solve problems (no more than two digits times two digits without technology).
Quiz 13	4.4 E	The student is expected to use division to solve problems (no more than one-digit divisors and three-digit dividends without technology).
Quiz 14	4.5 A	The student is expected to round whole numbers to the nearest ten, hundred, or thousand to approximate reasonable results in problem situations.
Quiz 15	4.5 B	The student is expected to use strategies including rounding and compatible numbers to estimate solutions to multiplication and division problems.
Objective 2: Patterns, Relationships, and Algebraic Thinking		
Quiz 16	4.6 A	The student is expected to use patterns and relationships to develop strategies to remember basic multiplication and division facts.
Quiz 17	4.6 B	The student is expected to use patterns to multiply by 10 and 100.
Quiz 18	4.7 A	The student is expected to describe the relationship between two sets of related data such as ordered pairs in a table.
Objective 3: Geometry and Spatial Reasoning		
Quiz 19	4.8 A	The student is expected to identify and describe right, acute, and obtuse angles.
Quiz 20	4.8 B	The student is expected to identify and describe parallel and intersecting (including perpendicular) lines using pictorial models.
Quiz 21	4.8 C	The student is expected to use essential attributes to define two- and three-dimensional geometric figures.
Quiz 22	4.9 B	The student is expected to use translations, reflections, and rotations to verify that two shapes are congruent.
Quiz 23	4.9 C	The student is expected to use reflections to verify that a shape has symmetry.
Quiz 24	4.10 A	The student is expected to locate and name points on a number line using whole numbers, fractions such as halves and fourths, and decimals such as tenths.

Objective 4: Measurement		
Quiz 25	4.11 A	The student is expected to estimate and use measurement tools to determine length (including perimeter), area, capacity, and weight/mass using standard units SI (metric) and customary.
Quiz 26	4.11 B	The student is expected to perform simple conversions between different units of length, between different units of capacity, and between different units of weight within the customary measurement system.
Quiz 27	4.11 C	The student is expected to use models of standard cubic units to measure volume.
Quiz 28	4.12 A	The student is expected to use a thermometer to measure temperature and changes in temperature.
Objective 5: Probability and Statistics		
Quiz 29	4.13 A	The student is expected to use pictures to make generalizations about determining all possible combinations of a given set of data or of objects in a problem situation.
Quiz 30	4.13 B	The student is expected to interpret bar graphs.
Objective 6: Underlying Processes and Mathematical Tools		
Quiz 31	4.14 A	The student is expected to identify the mathematics in everyday situations.
Quiz 32	4.14 B	The student is expected to solve problems that incorporate understanding the problem, making a plan, carrying out the plan, and evaluating the solution for reasonableness.
Quiz 33	4.14 C	The student is expected to select or develop an appropriate problem-solving plan or strategy, including drawing a picture, looking for a pattern, systematic guessing and checking, acting it out, making a table, working a simpler problem, or working backwards to solve a problem.
Quiz 34	4.15 B	The student is expected to relate informal language to mathematical language and symbols.
Quiz 35	4.16 A	The student is expected to make generalizations from patterns or sets of examples and nonexamples.

Score Tracker

Objective 1: Numbers, Operations, and Quantitative Reasoning

Quiz 1	/6
Quiz 2	/6
Quiz 3	/4
Quiz 4	/5
Quiz 5	/5
Quiz 6	/6
Quiz 7	/6
Quiz 8	/5
Quiz 9	/5
Quiz 10	/6
Quiz 11	/7
Quiz 12	/6

Quiz 13	**/6**
Quiz 14	**/6**
Quiz 15	**/6**
TOTAL	**/85**

Objective 2: Patterns, Relationships, and Algebraic Thinking

Quiz 16	**/6**
Quiz 17	**/6**
Quiz 18	**/4**
TOTAL	**/16**

Objective 3: Geometry and Spatial Reasoning

Quiz 19	**/5**
Quiz 20	**/4**
Quiz 21	**/6**
Quiz 22	**/5**
Quiz 23	**/5**
Quiz 24	**/6**
TOTAL	**/31**

Objective 4: Measurement

Quiz 25	**/6**
Quiz 26	**/6**
Quiz 27	**/4**
Quiz 28	**/4**
TOTAL	**/20**

Objective 5: Probability and Statistics

Quiz 29	**/4**
Quiz 30	**/6**
TOTAL	**/10**

Objective 6: Underlying Processes and Mathematical Tools

Quiz 31	/6
Quiz 32	/6
Quiz 33	/5
Quiz 34	/6
Quiz 35	/5
TOTAL	/28

Mixed Quizzes

Quiz 36	/6
Quiz 37	/6
Quiz 38	/5
Quiz 39	/6
Quiz 40	/6
TOTAL	/29

Texas Test Prep Practice Test Book

For additional test prep, get the Texas Test Prep Practice Test Book. It contains 3 complete full-length STAAR Math practice tests. It's the perfect way for students to test their new and improved math skills in a test format that is exactly like the real Texas STAAR Math test.

Made in the USA
Charleston, SC
22 March 2012